James Orchard Halliwell-Phillipps

A hand-list of the drawings and engravings illustrative of the life of Shakespeare

Preserved at Hollingbury Copse, near Brighton

James Orchard Halliwell-Phillipps

A hand-list of the drawings and engravings illustrative of the life of Shakespeare
Preserved at Hollingbury Copse, near Brighton

ISBN/EAN: 9783337196448

Printed in Europe, USA, Canada, Australia, Japan

Cover: Foto ©Thomas Meinert / pixelio.de

More available books at **www.hansebooks.com**

A HAND-LIST.

Recipients of this little Volume would confer a great favour on the Compiler by informing him of any other old Views of Stratford-on-Avon and its neighbourhood, or of the various localities herein mentioned.

A HAND-LIST

OF

The Drawings and Engravings

ILLUSTRATIVE OF

THE LIFE OF SHAKESPEARE,

PRESERVED AT

HOLLINGBURY COPSE, NEAR BRIGHTON,

That quaint wigwam on the Sussex Downs which has the honour of sheltering more rarities connected with the personal and literary history of the Great Dramatist than are elsewhere to be found south of the Metropolis.

BRIGHTON:
FOR PRIVATE CIRCULATION ONLY.

MDCCCLXXXIV.

PREFACE.

It is very difficult to meet with pictorial illustrations of the Life of Shakespeare that belong to even a small antiquity. With the exception of two or three found in periodicals, and which are sufficiently common, any of the kind which were executed more than seventy years ago are of exceedingly rare occurrence. The Bodleian Library, so rich in English topography, has none; while in that enormous literary warehouse, the British Museum, there are hardly any of the slightest interest.

There are, indeed, only two large and important collections of drawings and engravings illustrative of Shakespearean biography. One of these, that now preserved at the Birth-Place, was formed by the late Mr. W. O. Hunt and myself in years gone by, when we ransacked Stratford-upon-Avon and its neighbourhood for every relic of the kind. The other, that now at Hollingbury Copse, is the result of purchases from other localities. Each collection is, at present, of unique interest, and is likely to remain so. It is not probable that another, of equal value to either, could now be formed.

But although this is not probable, there is no telling what the accidents of discovery may bring forth—in some forgotten portfolio, or in a find revealed by the disturbance of interior plasters. It is only about twelve years since that I purchased from my old friend, Mr. Joseph Lilly, the well-known bookseller of Garrick Street, a volume the inclusion of which, in itself alone, would have conferred a distinction on any such collection as that now briefly calendared. It was a copy of the first edition of Dugdale's Antiquities of Warwickshire, 1656, which had belonged to Richard Greene of Lichfield, a person who was intimately connected with Stratford-upon-Avon, and who had illustrated that fine old work with original drawings made by himself and others between the years 1760 and 1769. It was thus that I became possessed of the inestimable earliest representation of the Birth-Place known to exist, and of various sketches executed during that period, all of which are unique and most of extreme interest.

Amongst these and other noticeable articles may be mentioned,—Nos. 1 to 6 and 570 to 577, Fisher's original drawings of the paintings in the Guild Chapel, taken at the time of their discovery in 1804, and valuable as being more accurate than the engraved copies; Nos. 7 to 11, the London Arches of Triumph, 1604; Nos. 17, 18, 75, 150, 151, 155, 207, last century drawings and views of Stratford Church ; Nos. 28, 245, 545, Braun's plan of London, 1574 ; No. 35, Collier's rare plan of Windsor, 1742, showing Herne's Oak ; No. 45, a view of Charlecote, 1722 ; No. 65, Norden's original plan of Middlesex, c. 1593 ; Nos. 67, 666, 1069 to 1071, plans and drawings by John Jordan, a Stratfordian who died in 1809 ; Nos. 193, 737, the earliest known engravings of Shakespeare's Cliff near Dover, sketches by Hollar, c. 1640; No. 195, the oldest view of Herne's Oak ; No. 433, an early view of Charlecote ; No. 455, Winter's plan of Stratford, c. 1760; No. 506, a view of Stratford bridge, c. 1762 ; No. 563, a ground-plan of Stratford College, temp. Hen. 8, a remarkably curious relic preserved on the cover of a valuable early manuscript of local collections purchased in London at the sale of the Wheler library ; No. 652, a view of Stratford College taken in 1765 ; and No. 979, the rare contemporary engraved portrait of Shakespeare's friend, Lord Southampton. The collection is peculiarly rich in engraved views of the Shakespearean localities, especially in those of the Birth-Place and the Church.

But the gem of my collection is the engraving of Shakespeare by Droeshout, 1623, *in its original proof state before it was altered by an inferior hand into the vitiated form in which it has been so long familiar to the public.* This is the earliest engraved portrait of the great dramatist, and differs so materially from the later impressions that it gives a new and more pleasing idea of his features. Here we have the most reliable likeness of Shakespeare in existence, the only one which has not been injuriously tampered with, while, at the same time, the evidences of its genuineness and its antiquity are incontestable. Although it is not likely to be absolutely unique, it is certainly of the most excessive rarity, being the only copy that has yet been noticed.

The present collection is not the result of a mere desire for accumulation. It has been formed with the definite purpose of illustrating the Life of Shakespeare by representations of every morsel that could be found of his own contemporary England,—that is to say, of every object that he himself was likely to have seen. Deeply impressed by the rapidity with which these vestiges were disappearing, I engaged Mr. J. T. Blight, F.S.A., a very accomplished draughtsman, to make sketches in furtherance of this design during the years from 1862 to 1868. Not only was every corner of Stratford-upon-Avon and its neighbourhood explored, but we followed as far as we could the routes known to have been taken by the poet in his various journeys, anxiously searching for remains that could be positively assigned to his own times, and carefully excluding those which had passed through the hands of the modern restorer. A considerable proportion of the sketches then made are of objects that have since been either modernized or destroyed.

A large work on the lines above indicated could hardly fail to be welcome to the student, but, as is so often the case, the time occupied in gathering together the necessary artistic and literary material has practically excluded the collector himself from the opportunity of making an effective use of his accumulations. As our Brighton whip, in the old days of coaching, used to say,—" tempus will fudgit,"—and it has fudgited with me until there is but a little working slice of it left. That slice is insufficient for the due execution of such an undertaking. In a very few years, half a century will have elapsed since my first work on Shakespeare was published, and the termination of that period must also, if I survive, be that of my student work. If the fate of the Archbishop of Grenada is to be escaped, this should be the resolve not merely of those who have traversed the higher walks of literature, but of the lesser votaries who, like myself, lay claim to nothing beyond a capacity for research and the ability of utilizing its products.

Little autobiographical reflections of this kind might anyhow be excused in a privately-printed brochure of very limited circulation, but they are in fact given as the most effectual method of advising a younger enthusiast that he can, without lack of courtesy to the originator, carry out an important design. When such a one arises with the large means that will be requisite to complete the work in a satisfactory manner, the artistic materials catalogued in the following pages cannot fail to prove of essential service.

J. O. HALLIWELL-PHILLIPPS.

Hollingbury Copse, Brighton.
3 March, 1884.

A HAND-LIST.

1. The Guild Chapel.—The Last Judgment, or the Day of Doom, copied by Fisher in 1804 from paintings discovered on the west side of the wall that divides the nave and chancel. The original drawing, coloured.

2. The Guild Chapel.—Sketch-plans of the north and south sides of the Chancel, showing the situation of the paintings. Also, a coloured sketch of the paintings at the Vicar's door. Fisher del. The originals.

3. The Guild Chapel.—The metrical inscriptions on Earth found in the painting on the west wall of the nave, beneath the death of Becket. The original facsimile made on a large scale by Fisher.

4. The Guild Chapel.—Saint Modwena and St. Edmund the King, paintings in the westernmost niches on the south and north sides of the nave. The original drawings by Fisher.

5. The Guild Chapel.—The Visit of the Queen of Sheba to Solomon, and the victory of Constantine over Mexentius. Fisher's original coloured copies of paintings on the north side of the chancel.

6. The Guild Chapel.—An Angel with admonitory verses, a painting on the west wall and south of the entrance, beneath the representation of the death of Becket. Fisher del.

7-11. The Arches of Triumph erected in honor of King James the First at his Majesties entrance and passage through his honourable Citty of London, upon the 15th day of March, 1603-4. Five of the original very rare contemporary engravings by William Kip, Stephen Harrison, and another, including the one which has the view of London. There is authentic record evidence that Shakespeare was in the procession on this interesting occasion.

12. An exact Prospect of the City of Rochester, taken from Finsbery Windmill by Ja. Collins. Twenty-seven inches in length.

13. The North-West Prospect of the City of

Rochester. S. and N. Buck del. et sculpt., March 25th, 1738.

14. The Chancel of Stratford - upon - Avon Church, showing the new timber roof designed by Harvey Eginton, architect, and executed under the direction of the committee of the Royal Shakespeare Club, 1837.

15. A south-east view of the exterior of Stratford Church. A large original drawing in water-colours by J. C. Buckler, 1823.

16. A large view of the western end of the exterior of Stratford Church, c. 1830. Name of artist unknown.

17. A large pen-and-ink drawing of the exterior of Stratford Church, showing the tower and southern side of the western end, executed about the year 1762. This and the next drawing were in Richard Greene's illustrated copy of Dugdale, but it may be suspected, from the style, that they were not executed by him.

18. A large pen-and-ink drawing of the north exterior side of Stratford Church, executed about the year 1762.

19. The Chancel of Stratford Church—the Tomb of Shakspeare—drawn by W. H. Hutchinson, engraved by W. Radclyffe. Published at Birmingham, Dec. 3rd, 1827.

20. The Font at which Shakespeare was baptized. A coloured lithograph by J. Salmon from a drawing by Mrs. Dighton. Published at Stratford-on-Avon, June 1st, 1835.

21. The Mappe of Norfolke, Svffolke, Cambridgeshire, Bedford, Hartford, Buckingham, Oxford, Northampton, Warwick, Huntington and Lecestershires, and Rutland, part of Lincolne, Nottingham, Darbye, Glocester and Barckshires, and of the County of Essex.—This map was engraved at least as early as 1644. The main roads are marked by double lines and the cross-roads by single ones. This is a large and important map.

22. Worcestershire, Described by Christopher Saxton, augmented and published by Iohn Speede, citizen of London, and are there to be solde in Popes-heade Alley against the Exchange by John Sudbury and George Humble. Anno Domini

1610.—Jodocus Hondius cælavit.—No roads marked. There is a plan of Worcester in the right-hand corner.

23. The Road from Glocester to Coventrey, by Iohn Ogilby, Esq., His Majesties Cosmographer, containing 58 miles 2 furlongs, vizt, from Glocester to Cheltenham 9 miles 4, to Winchcomb 7 m., to Campden 11.' 4, to Stratford 11.' 3, to Warwick 8.' 3, to Coventrey 10.' 4. 1675.

24. Warwici Comitatvs Descriptio, quam primus ædidit Christophorus Saxton anno 1576, nunc de integro correcta, aucta et restituta ; cui adduntur (præter 60 locos qui priore desiderabantur) singula hundreda, viæ notiores, in vsum itinerantium accomodatæ, et alia non infimæ notæ nonnulla, anno 1603.—Near the corner is—Printed and sovld by P. Stent. —This is the earliest map of Warwickshire in which the roads are marked, Stent having, I believe, put or stamped his name as publisher to a plate of older date than the period at which he flourished.

25. The Counti of Warwick, the Shire Towne and Citie of Coventre described. Per-

formed by Iohn Speede and are to by solde in Popes-heade ally against the Exchange by Iohn Sudbury and George Humble. Cum privilegio. 1610.—No roads marked. There is a plan of Warwick in the left-hand corner and one of Coventry in the right.

26. A later edition of the last-mentioned engraving, in which the roads are introduced. Performed by Iohn Speede, and are to be sold by Thomas Bassett in Fleetstreet and Richard Chiswell in St. Pauls Churchyard.

27. The Map of Oxfordshire newly delineated and after a new manner. From Plot's Natural History of Oxfordshire, 1677.— Only the Roman roads marked. This map includes a portion of Berkshire.

28. Londinum Feracissimi Angliæ Regni Metropolis. Braun's plan, 1574. Not coloured.

29. A New Description of Kent divided into the fyue Lathes therof, and subdivided into Baylywickes and Hundredes, with the parishe Churches conteyned within euery of the same Hundredes. All which, for better vnderstandinge, are

distinguished with varyetye of coloures: Comprehendinge as well the Cities, the vsuall Market townes and the Portes with their members lying in Kent: As also such of the howses of the Nobylitie and Gentrye as the Plott coulde conueniently receaue. Wherin moreover the nature of the soyle, whether playne, hyllye or wooddye, is more diligentlye observed, and the tractes of Ryuers, Rylles and creekes, with the trendinge of the sea-shore, be more naturally described then heretofore it hath ben done. By the travayle of Phil: Symonson of Rochester, gent. Printed and sovld by P. Stent at the White Horse in giltspure street, 1659.—At the top is a view of Dover by Hollar, and one of Rye by Sir Anthony Van Dyck, the latter showing the sea up to the town.

30. The Royall Palace and Town of Windsor.— Le Palais Royal et Ville de Windsor.— Printed and Sold by Thos. Bowles, Print and Map Seller next to the Chapter House in St. Paul's Church Yard, London.

31. Wigorniensis comitatus cum Warwicensi,

necnon Coventriæ Libertas.—Amstelodami ; apud Ioannem Iansonium.

32. The South Prospect of Reading in the County of Berks.—S. and N. Buck del. et sc., 1734.

33. A large view of the Town, Castle and Parks of Windsor, dedicated "to her Most Serene and Most Sacred Majesty Anne, by the grace of God, Queen of Great Britain, France and Ireland, &c." Printed and Sold by Henry Overton at the White Horse without Newgate.

34. Plan du Chateau et Parc de Windsor, dans la Conté de Berk, a 20 Milles de Londres, renferment une des maisons et jardins du Duc de Marlborough ; tres exatement Levé et Gravé par J. Rocque, 1738.

35. A Plan of the Town and Castle of Windsor and Little Park, and the Town and College of Eton, Survey'd and Drawn by W. Collier. Publish'd according to Act of Parliament by W. Collier at Eton, 1742, by whom Lands are Survey'd and Maps drawn of the same in the best and cheapest manner. Sold by J. Pine, Engraver in Old Bond Street, and T.

Bakewell, Printseller in Fleet Street. Engrav'd by J. Pine.—The very rare original engraving, being the earliest plan of Windsor Park in which Herne's Oak is noticed.

36. Another copy, with slight variations, of that portion of the same plan which includes Herne's Oak.

37. A Mapp of Warwickshire, describing the Boundaries and Divisions, the Rivers, Brooks and Rills, the Roman Roads and Stations, the Parish Churches and Chapels. From an actual Survey made in the year 1725 by Henry Beighton, Fellow of the Royal Society, 1729; containing the Roads in measur'd and computed Miles, depopulated places, Seats of the Nobility and Gentry, Chaces, Parkes, K.^{s} Houses, Baronies, Monastaries, Castles, Battels, Garisons, Mines and Medicinal Waters. I. Mynde sc.

38. A Map of Hemlingford Hund., reduc'd from an Actual Survey made in the year 1725 by Hen. Beighton.

39. A Map of Warwickshire by Robert Morden.

Sold by Abel Swale, Awnsham and Iohn Churchil.—Roads marked.

40. A large drawing of Windsor Castle, the town and river, by Belanger. This was in the Moltena sale, 1817.

41. A View of the Antient Royal Palace, called Placentia, in East Greenwich. Publish'd according to Act of Parliament, April 23, 1767, sumpt. Societ. Antiquar.

42. A Prospect of the House att Windsor belonging to his Grace, Charles Beauclerck, Duke of St. Albans, Earle of Burford and Baron of Heddington, Capt. of the Hon.[ble] Band of Gentlemen Pensioners, Marshall and Surveyour of the Hawkes to his Maj.[tie], and one of the Gentlemen of his Maj.[ts] Bed Chamber. L. Knyff de. I. Kip scu. This engraving includes curious and interesting views of the towns of Windsor and Eton. Circa 1720.

43. Windsor Castle. Le Chasteau de Windsor. L. Knyff del. I. Kip sculp.—This view shows a good many of the old houses at Windsor about the year 1720.

44. The Royal Palace of Windsor. Le Palais

Royal de Windsor. H. Gravelot delin. J. Major sculp. Printed for John Bowles at the Black Horse in Cornhill. —This view includes a portion of the town. Several reduced copies of it were subsequently published.

45. The East Prospect of Charlecote in Warwickshire, the Seat of the Reverend Wm. Lucy, Esq., 1722. H. Beighton delin. 1722. E. Kirkall sculp.

46. Prospect of Windsor Castle and Towne from South S. West. Prospect of the same Castle from West South West. Prospect of it from West and by South. W. Hollar delin. et sculp.

47. Shakespeare's Cliff, Dover, from a Sketch taken in 1843. F. W. Fairholt sc.

48. The Shakspeare Cliff, Dover. A large etching by one M. S., 1820.

49. Oxonium nobile Angliæ oppidum, septentrionalem Tamesis ripam elegantissimo atque salubri situ illustrat. Depingeb. Georg. Hoefnagle. 1574.

50. Vindesorivm celeberrimum Angliæ castrum locus amoenissimus ; ædificia magnifica ; artificiosa Regum sepulchra, et illustris

Garetteriorum equitum Societas memorabile reddunt. Depingebat Georgius Hoefnagle. Cum priuilegio. 1574.

51. The Old Stabling of the Three Pigeons, Brentford, the inn frequented by Shakespeare and Ben Jonson. Drawn and Etched by W. N. Wilkins, June, 1848.

52. Windsor Castle and Park. 1818.

53. Datchet Bridge upon the river Thames. Wm. Oram delin., July 25, 1745.

54. A large and very curious sepia drawing of the Castle and part of the town, executed about the year 1640.

55. Windsor Castle. W. Hollar delineavit et sculpsit.—This is a curious view, showing part of the ancient town in interesting detail.

56. The College in Stratford-upon-Avon, in the County of Warwick, the Seat of the Combe's, the Clopton's and the Keyte's, with their Arms and Quarterings.—A large view taken about the year 1810.

57. Prospect of Windsor Castle from the North. Christopher Wren delineavit. W. Hollar fecit, 1667.—A very interest-

ing engraving, including detailed views of many of the old houses.

58. A Map of Knightlow Hundred, reduced from an actual Survey made, in the year 1725, by Henry Beighton.

59. The Mapp of Kineton Hundred. Ro. Vaughan sculp. From Dugdale's Warwickshire, 1656.

60. The Mapp of Knightlow Hvndred. From Dugdale's Warwickshire, 1656.

61. The Mapp of Warwickshire, containing the Rivers, Roman wayes, Parish Churches and Chapells. From Dugdale's Warwickshire, 1656.

62. A Map of Barlichway Hundred, reduced from an actual Survey made, in the year 1725, by Henry Beighton.

63. Warwici Comitatus, a Cornauiis olim inhabitatus. Christophorus Saxton descripsitt, William Kip sculpsitt. — No roads marked.

64. The Mapp of Hemlingford Hundred. Ro. Vaughan sculpsit. From Dugdale's Warwickshire, 1656.

65. Norden's original Plan of Middlesex, on a much larger scale and with numerous variations from the published engraving of 1593 (See No. 110).—This interesting survey was executed for Queen Elizabeth, Norden referring to "Your Magesties howses" in the list of objects he has attached to the plan, and the Queen's arms being depicted in the left-hand corner.

₊ Norden was the first English surveyor who had any kind of pretension to scientific accuracy. His original manuscript plans are of great rarity, the present one of Middlesex and that of Essex, the latter in the possession of the Marquis of Salisbury at Hatfield, being the only ones known in private libraries.

66. A Map of Kineton Hundred, reduced from an actual Survey made, in the year 1725, by Henry Beighton of Griff in Warwickshire, F.R.S.

67. An Ichnography of the Borough of Stratford-upon-Avon and the Village of Old Stratford, in the County of Warwick. A large original plan made by Jordan about the year 1780.

68. A Mapp of the County of Middlesex, with its Hundreds, by Ric. Blome, by His Maj. comand. 1673.

69. Middlesex olima Trinobantibvs habitata. Johannes Norden descripsit. From Camden, 1607.—No roads shown.

70. A large plan of Oxford and a small view of the town, 1649. An engraving of foreign execution.

71. A Mapp of Warwickshire with its Hvndreds, by Ric. Blome. By His Majesty's Comand, 1673.—No roads shown.

72. A Map of Middlesex, described by Iohn Norden, augmented by I. Speed, sold by Henry Overton at the White Horse without Newgate, London.—The main roads shown.

73. The Ground Plott of Warwick. W. Hollar fecit, 1654. From Dugdale's Warwickshire, 1656.

74. The Mapp of Barlichway Hundred. Ro. Vaughan sculp. From Dugdale's Warwickshire, 1656.

75. A Ground Plan of Stratford Church, including that of the Charnel-house, with a Scale of Feet. Copied by Richard Greene, in the year 1765, from a drawing by S. Winter.

76. A New Map, containing the Towns, Gentlemen's Houses, Villages and other Remarks round London, as from London to Windsor, Ware, Chelmsford, the Hope, Tunbridge, Guildford, &c. Maed and sold by H. Moll in Vanly's Court in Blackfryers.—A very elaborate map showing the main roads.

77. A large sketch of Shakespeare's crab-tree and surrounding scenery. Believed to be a copy of an earlier view.

78-79. Two Views of the Crab-tree copied by Blight from rude originals, taken about the year 1810, in the Stratford-upon-Avon Museum.

80. The Blue Boar Inn at Leicester, the house at which Richard the Third is said to have slept the night before the battle of Bosworth. Ireland, 1795. This wood-engraving is admitted into the collection as a specimen of an old timbered house in a town that Shakespeare is believed to have visited.

81. The Ancient House in the High Street, Stratford-on-Avon. Rock and Co., London.

82. The Shakespeare Monument, Stratford-upon-Avon. Rock and Co., London.

83. The Hall, Charlecote House, Stratford-on-Avon. Rock and Co., London. Ward, Stratford, Nov. 10th, 1849.

84. The Church and Avon Bank, Stratford-on-Avon. Published by J. Ward. F. Eginton sc., Birm.

85. Charlecote Hall, the Residence of George Lucy, esq. Rock and Co., London.

86. The Shakespear Chair. Hogarth pinx. 1799.

87. Iohn Combe, taken from his Monument in the Church of Stratford-upon-Avon. Drawn and Etch'd by S. Harding, 1793.

88. The Church of Stratford-upon-Avon, taken from the Water. T. Thornton del. Medland sculp. Published Nov. 1, 1793, by E. and S. Harding, Pall Mall.

89. The Interior of Stratford Church, a large sketch by J. T. Blight, c. 1862.

90. Deale Castle. W. Hollar delin.

91. An Elizabethan Inn at Rochester, Exterior and Interior. F. W. Fairholt, F.S.A., sc.

92. The New Place Chapel, Guildhall, &c. Drawn by R. B. Wheler. Engraved by F. Eginton, Birm. 1806.

93. Stratford-upon-Avon Church. C. F. Green lithog.—Published about the year 1820.

94. The Combe Effigy in Stratford Church, a pencil drawing by Blight. The effigy is complete, but the surroundings are unfinished.

95. The Cottage at Shottery wherein Anne Hathaway (Shakspeare's Wife) resided. C. F. Green del. A lithograph of the exterior, with two figures in the foreground and a woman at the entrance, published about the year 1820.

96. Shakespeare Cliff. Tomkins del. Sparrow sc.

97. Stratford-on-Avon Church, a coloured print. This view was taken from the river-side opposite to Avon Bank.

98. Part of Windsor Castle and adjoining houses. Publish'd as the Act directs by P. Sandby, St. Georges Row, Oxford Turnpike, Feb. 1st., 1780. P. Sandby fecit.

99. Stratford-upon-Avon Church. Rock and Co., London. A view of the northern side and western end.

100. Stratford-upon-Avon Church. Laney lithog. Pub?. by J. Ward. A view of the northern side and western end.

101. New Place, Stratford-on-Avon, Residence of Shakspeare. Rock and Co., London. No. 828. This shows the later New Place, the eastern end of the Guild Chapel, and a small portion of the Grammar School.

102. Shakspere's Crab Tree. C. Fisher, 1830.

103. Herne's Oak, Windsor Park. Pub. for S. Ireland, May 1, 1799.

104. Daisy Hill Farm House, the Keeper's Lodge at Charlecot. C. Fisher, 1830.

105. Windsor and the Little Park, A.D. 1607, from a Plan by John Norden. F. W. Fairholt sc.

106. 107. The South Side of Windsor Castle. Prospect of the Castle from the S.E.— Two long views by Hollar, c. 1670.

The first of these views contains, I believe, the earliest representation of the Church at which Anne Page was married.

108. The prospect of Warwick from Coventre Roade on the North-east part of the Towne.—The prospect of it from London road on the south side of the Towne.—From Dugdale, 1656.

109. The Mapp of Canterbury. From Somner's Antiquities of Canterbury, 4to. 1640.

110. Myddlesex. Iohannes Norden Angl. descripsit, 1593.—This plan shows all the main roads. It is the diminutive published engraving, a larger and more elaborate original plan being in this collection. See No. 65.

111. The Monumental Effigy of Shakspeare, engraved by I. S. Agar from an original Drawing by A. Wivell in the possession of John Cordy, esq. London, Published Nov. 1825, by Geo. Lawford, Saville Place.

112. The Monumental Effigy of Shakespeare. F. W. Fairholt, del. et sc., 1852. On India-paper.

113. 114. Shakespeare's Tomb. Stratford-on-Avon, Published June 1st, 1835, by Mrs. P. Dighton, and Ackermann and Co., 96, Strand, London. Drawn by Mrs. P.

Dighton. Printed by Lefevre and Kohler, 52, Newman Street. Lithographed by J. Salmon.—Two copies, one coloured and the other plain.

115. The Monumental Effigy of Shakespeare. Published by F. and E. Ward, Stratford-on-Avon. C. Graf lith., 1, Great Castle Street, London. 1851.

116. Shakspeare. Engraved by T. A. Dean, after a Drawing by A. Wivell, from the bust by Gerard Johnson. London, Published, 1827, by A. Wivell, 40, Castle Street East.

117. The Interior of the Chancel of Stratford Church, as seen from the southern exterior through an open door. A coloured lithograph.

118. Sir Thomas Lucy, from a picture in the hall at Charlecote. A pencil copy by Blight from a pen-and-ink sketch by F. W. Fairholt.

119. The Monumental Effigy. G. Vertue sculp. 1725.

120. The Monumental Effigy. A sketch by Blight, 1864, from Bullock's cast.

121 A very clumsy sketch of the same cast, engraved by W. T. Fry. Published November 1st, 1817, by T. Cadell and W. Davies, Strand, London.

122. The Monumental Effigy, drawn by Mr. John Boaden from the Stratford Bust. Engraved by E. Scriven. 1825.

123. Shakspeare's Monument. Drawn by R. B. Wheler. Engraved by F. Eginton, Birm. 1806.

124. Mr. William Shakspeare his true Effigies, engraved by Wm. Ward, A.R.A., from a painting by Thos. Phillips, esq., R.A., after a Cast by G. Bullock from the Bust at Stratford-on-Avon. 1816.

125. The Monumental Effigy of Shakespeare, "In the North wall of the Chancell is this Monument fixt." With the inscriptions on the monument and grave-stone. From Dugdale, 1656.

126. Sir Thomas Lucy from the Effigy at Charlecote. A pencil copy by Blight of a sketch by F. W. Fairholt.

127. 128. Two diminutive views, one a full and the other a side one, of the monumental

effigy.   E. Blore del.   Thompson sc. 1814.

129. Jo: Barclaius, ob. 1621. An engraved portrait of this author, who is represented in a costume very similar to that in which Shakespeare appears in the monumental effigy. See this print described in Wivell's Inquiry into the Shakspeare Portraits, 1827, pp. 64-66.

130. 131. Effigies in the Clopton Chapel, Stratford-on-Avon. Two beautifully executed pencil drawings by J. T. Blight, 1864.

132. A diminutive view of London, from the title-page of Sir Richard Baker's Chronicle, 1665. W. Marshall sculpsit.—Evidently copied from an earlier view, as it shows two of the Southwark theatres.

133. The Droeshout portrait of Shakespeare, 1623, engraved by Blight from the proof copy of that engraving.

134. A View at the Western end of Uxbridge. J. Stokes del.   J. Gleadah sc.

135. The pulpit at Alderminster, said to have been formerly in Stratford Church and to have been the one presented to the

latter by John Hall, Shakespeare's son-in-law. A pencil sketch by Blight.

136. The roof of the nave of Stratford-on-Avon Church, from a painting taken before the alterations of 1836.

137. Ruins of the Roman pharos and first Christian Church within Dover Castle. A pen-and-ink sketch by F. W. Fairholt, c. 1849.

138. Elizabetha Regina. Engraved from a painting by John de Critz, and published by Henry Holland in 1620.

139. The cellar at Shakespeare's Birth-Place, a water-colour by Blight, 1865.

140. A large unfinished pencil sketch of the exterior of Stratford Church, by J. T. Blight.

141. A large pencil sketch of Stratford Church, taken by Blight from the eastern side of the river.

142. A sketch of Chapel Lane, showing the cottage on the site of Getley's (afterwards Shakespeare's) copyhold estate. A recent copy of an earlier view.

143. An engraved Portrait of the Earl of Essex,

who was beheaded in 1601, and who was one of the patrons of Shakespeare's company. From an original painting then preserved at Essex House. Published by Holland in 1620.

144. Campden House, near London. 1795.

145. The Church of the Holy Trinity, Stratford-on-Avon, a sketch by Blight, 1863, from Mr. W. O. Hunt's garden on the river-side.

146. The western end of Stratford Church, a pencil sketch by Blight, 1863.

147. A view of Stratford Church from the Old Town, the ancient stocks in the foreground. A copy of a sketch in the Wheler collection.

148. A sketch of an ancient chair preserved in what is called Mary Arden's house at Wilmecote. Taken by Blight, 1863.

149. The Interior of the Sexton's Cottage at Stratford-on-Avon, a curious old room, c. 1830. A copy only.

150. 151. An East View of the Collegiate Church of Stratford-upon-Avon. A South-East view of the Col. Church of

Stratford.—These drawings were made in or before the year 1763, and show the designs for a new steeple by Timothy Lightholder. They were, no doubt, although not so stated, made by Richard Greene in 1762, as may be ascertained by comparing them with No. 155.

152. Backs of old timber buildings in High Street, Stratford-on-Avon, the fronts of which have been modernized. Sketched by Blight, 1863.

153. Articles called Shakespeare's Jug and Cane, pencil sketches of the originals in the possession of Mrs. Fletcher, of Gloucester.

154. A water-colour sketch, by Blight, of an ancient carved oak court-cupboard, formerly in the house said to have belonged to the Ardens at Wilmecote.

155. A South West View of the Collegiate Church, Stratford-upon-Avon. R. Greene del. 1762.—A carefully drawn and extremely interesting early view of the church.

156. An elegantly executed sketch of Stratford Church, taken, about the year 1820, from the northern bank of the river.

157. Shakespeare's Birth-Place. An engraving issued by the London Shakespeare Committee in 1847, and stated by them to be "from a recent drawing."

158. Mortlack Church, c. 1740. See No. 164. Shakespeare's company were at Mortlake in 1603.

159. Shakespeare's Birth-Place, as it appeared in 1788. A copy engraved for and issued by the London Shakespeare Committee in 1847.

160. The Room in which Shakspeare was born. T. G. Flowers, Edinburgh. c. 1840.

161. A sketch of a rush candle-stick, one of those in use in the country in Shakespeare's time, from a specimen discovered at Stratford-on-Avon.

162. Shakespeare's Birth-Place. Exterior. T. G. Flowers, Edinburgh. c. 1840.

163. Oxford Castle and some old houses near it. A sketch taken by Blight in 1864.

164. A View of the Village of Mortlake, a copy of an engraving by M. Chatelaine, c. 1740. See No. 158.

165. The Royal Pallace and Town of Windsor. Published by Cox, 1720.

166. The Ground Plot of Kenilworth Castle. From Dugdale, 1656.

167. Ann Hathaway's Cottage, Shottery. Exterior. Published by F. and E. Ward.

168. An engraved portrait of Frederick, Duke of Wirtemberg, the Duke de Jarmany of the Merry Wives of Windsor, published in Germany in 1602.

169. Stratford-upon-Avon Church, architectural view without the foliage. T. G. Flowers, Edinburgh. c. 1840. Published by F. and E. Ward.

170. Datchet Mead and Windsor Park, A.D. 1686, from the Original in the Sutherland Collection. F. W. Fairholt sc.

171. A Map of Middlesex, by Robert Morden at the Atlas in Cornhill. 1724.

172. A Map of Warwickshire, by Robert Morden. 1720.

173. Timbered House at Charlecote. 1863.

174. A Plan of Warwicke, xvii. Cent.

175. Charlecote House. C. Fisher, 1830.

176. A Plan of Worcester, from Speed, 1614.

177. Shakspeare's House as it appeared in 1788. From the Penny Magazine, September the 1st, 1832.

178. A sketch by Blight, 1864, of a bridge on the road between Hillingdon and Uxbridge, the arches of which are of great antiquity. This bridge would have been passed over by Shakespeare in his journeys between London and Stratford.

179. A sketch of a box made of crab-tree wood, and pretended to have belonged to one John Jordan of Stratford-on-Avon in 1646.

180. Windsor Castle, with part of the town, the river in the fore-ground. Cox, 1720.

181. Map of Berkshire. Camden, 1607.

182. 183. Two coloured views, taken by Blight in 1864, of the ancient cellar at the Crown Inn, Rochester. Interesting medieval work. This tavern has since been either pulled down or completely modernized.

184. A water-colour drawing of Shakespeare's crab-tree, as it appeared about the year 1822. A recent copy.

185. Windsor Castle. A water-colour drawing made about the year 1780. Artist's name unknown.

186. A copy, in water-colour, of an oil painting, executed about the year 1690, of Windsor Castle, unique as showing the houses in the river, and the entrance of the lane through which Falstaff was carried in the buck-basket. The large original painting, formerly in my possession, I gave many years ago to the Birth-Place Museum.

187. Windsor Castle and Park. Drawn by J. Hakewill. Engraved by W. Woolnoth.

188. Pershore, Worcestershire. Sam. Ireland del., 1792.

189. Stratford Church, &c. Sam. Ireland del., 1792. This engraving shows also the river and the old mill.

190. Windsor Castle and Little Park. The royal carriage and attendants in the foreground. W. Hollar fecit, 1644.

191. Richmond Palace. M. Van de Gucht sculp.

192. Eton and its Bridge. An etching, 1809.

193. The Clyff of Dover. An etching by Hollar, c. 1640. Now called Shakespeare's Cliff.

194. Herne's Oak. T. Thornton del. Medland sculpsit. Published June 17, 1792, by E. Harding.

195. "A View of Herne's Oak in the Little Park at Windsor," with part of Queen Elizabeth's Walk. This original sketch, made by Hayman Rooke, an accurate topographer, about the year 1770, is the most interesting early drawing of the oak known to exist.

196. Two Prospects of Tamworth, co. Warwick. From Dugdale, 1656.

197. A View of the Castle, Town and Cliffe of Dover, c. 1780.

198. Shakspeare Cliff, Dover. Drawn by S. Owen. Engraved by W. B. Cooke. London, Published June 1, 1816, by J. Murray, Albemarle Street.

199. Dover, with Shakespeare's Cliff in the Distance. I. Nixon del. Sparrow sc. Pub. by E. Harding, Sep. 10, 1791.

200. A View of Broom, co. Warwick, the

"Beggarly Broom" of the well-known verses. An original sketch by the Rev. Richard Jago, Vicar of Snitterfield, c. 1778.

201. Old Houses at Eton. Drawn by S. Owen. Engraved by W. B. Cooke. Published Feb. 1, 1849.

202. The ancient carved porch and gateway at the Crown Inn, Rochester, sketched by Blight in 1863. Now pulled down.

203. The ancient bridge at Islip, co. Oxon. A pencil sketch by Blight, 1864.

204. A sketch of the ancient Register Book of Stratford-on-Avon, showing the old binding and the clasps.

205. A sketch of an ancient Bible preserved in the Parish Church of Stratford-on-Avon.

206. Herne's Oak, 1788. A. E. H. pinxit. G. E. H. fecit. An etching.

207. Borealis Prospectus Ecclesiæ Stratfordiæ Super Avon in Comitatu Warwicenci. J. Gwin sc. Viro Reverendo Josepho Greene, Regiæ Scholæ in Stratfordia Moderatori, humillime inscribitur. c. 1740.—This is the earliest engraved view of the Church known to exist.

208. An effigy in the Clopton Chapel, Stratford-on-Avon, sketched by Blight in 1864.

209. A sketch of the old font in Stratford Church, taken by Blight in 1864.

210. A doorway south side of the chancel of Stratford Church, sketched in 1864.

211. A sketch from the sedilia in the Chapel of St. Thomas, Stratford-upon-Avon.

212. An arch in the interior of the South Transept of Stratford Church, sketched by Blight.

213. An architectural moulding in the Clopton Chapel in Stratford Church, sketched by Blight in 1865.

214. An exceedingly curious termination of the hood-moulding of a window on the north side of the chancel of Stratford Church, sketched by Blight in 1866.

215. An outline sketch by Blight, 1863, of part of the tower staircase in Stratford Church.

216. 217. Small mediæval figures in Stratford Church.

218. The entrance to Stratford Churchyard, showing the wooden bars on the ground

to keep pigs from entering. A copy of an original sketch in the Saunders collection.

219—222. Four original sketches taken by Blight in 1863, of objects in the interior and on the exterior of Stratford Church.

223. A stone over the south window of transept in Stratford Church, and remains of mosaic pavement on the altar steps, copied from drawings by R. B. Wheler.

224—238. Fifteen original sketches, taken by Blight in 1863 and 1866, of objects in the interior and on the exterior of Stratford Church.

239. A view of the Church and village of Hillingdon, sketched by Blight in 864. This village is on the old road between Stratford-on-Avon and London.

240. An outline sketch by Blight of a window in Stratford Church, 1863.

241. A sketch of the inside of the Charnel House, Stratford Church, looking south, copied from a drawing by R. B. Wheler.

242. An outline sketch by Blight of the south door in the south aisle of Stratford Church.

243. A very perfect specimen of a small timbered building of the sixteenth century at Little Alne, co. Warwick, a place where some of the poet's connexions once resided. Sketched by Blight in August, 1863.

244. Cantvaria, vrbs fertilis simæ Angliæ celebris, Archiepiscopati sede, commendata. A curious plan of Canterbury, published by Braun in 1574.

245. Braun's large plan of London, 1574, a plain uncoloured copy with variations from the other one, No. 28.

246. A north-west view of Windsor Castle, with part of the town. Drawn and etch'd by J. Farington, R.A.

247. Windsor. Drawn by P. Daschkaw, 1780. P. Sandby del.

248. Datchet Bridge near Windsor. P. Sandby pinxit. E. Rooker sculp., 1774.

249. Windsor Bridge, and a small number of the houses in Windsor and Eton. An etching published Oct. 10, 1790, by W. Payne, Thornhaugh-street, Bedford Square.

250. Herne's Oak, Windsor Little Park. W.

Bromet, F.S.A.   C. Hollis sc.   An impression on large paper.

251. Windsor Castle, engraved in imitation of a highly interesting tinted Drawing by Wenceslaus Hollar in the possession of the publisher. Published Feb. 1st, 1828, by W. B. Tiffin, 3, Haymarket.

252. North View of Holland House.   1795.

253. A View of Acton from the South West. Royce sc.

254. South View of Holland House.   1795.

255. A Perspective View of the City of Rochester, showing a large number of the old houses.   Engrav'd for the Royal Magazine.

256. 257. Prospects of Dover and Banbury. 1724.   Stukeley delin.   Toms et E. Kirkall sculp.

258. Herne's Oak, 1788.   A lithographic copy, published in 1820.

259. The North Prospect of Trinity Church, Stratford-upon-Avon.   R. Hickes fecit, 1737.   A recent copy of an old drawing.

260. The left-hand cover of the old Register

Book of Stratford-on-Avon; a copy of a sketch by Fairholt.

261. Sedilia in Stratford Church, a pencil sketch by Blight taken in 1863.

262. The Church at Barton-on-the-Heath, a sketch taken by Blight on the 6th of October, 1864. This place was the residence of the Lamberts, who were connexions of the poet.

263—273. Eleven original sketches, by Blight, illustrative of Shakespeare's journeys between Stratford and London, viz., Tetsworth, West Wickham, the Crown Inn at Oxford, Stokenchurch, the Three Pigeons, Wheatley, Islip and Adderbury.

274. A large recumbent effigy in the Clopton Chapel, Stratford-on-Avon, sketched by Blight in 1864.

275. The upper part of an old pulpit formerly in Stratford Church. From an old painting made before the alterations of 1836.

276. The ancient bridge at Drunken Bidford, a copy by Blight of a sketch made about the year 1810.

277. The wooden cornice in the lower room

(now destroyed) of the old Crown Inn, Rochester, sketched by Blight in 1864.

278. Recumbent effigies of a gentleman and his wife, sketched by Blight from the originals in the Clopton Chapel, Stratford-on-Avon.

279. A recent copy of a view of Shakespeare's Crab-tree taken by C. F. Green in 1823.

280. Church Street, Oxford. A sketch, 1864.

281. A sketch of the roof of Stratford Church looking towards the tower. From a painting executed before the alterations of 1836.

282. The ancient bridge at Wixford, a copy of a sketch taken about the year 1810.

283. Curious old timbered houses in Bridge Lane, Warwick, one bearing the date of 1568. A sketch by F. W. Fairholt taken in 1847.

284—294. Eleven sketches, taken in 1864 by Blight, of localities illustrative of the journeys of Shakespeare, viz., Postcombe, Wheatley, Burmington, Uxbridge, Pershore, Acton, Steeple Aston, Oxford, Deddington, Banbury and Beaconsfield.

295. The Charnel House from Greene's view of Stratford Church. A recent copy.

296. A view of the Royal Palace at Windsor, 1765. A few of the houses in the town are shown.

297. Effigies in the North Isle and in the Clopton Chapel, Stratford Church. From Dugdale, 1656.

298. Interior of the Chancel of Stratford Church, showing Shakspeare's and other Monuments. Drawn by J. P. Neale. Engraved by H. Le Keux. 1824.

299. A pen-and-ink sketch taken by Fairholt, in 1849, of a timbered house, dated 1576, in the High Street, Birmingham.

300. An original tracing made by the elder Ireland, about the year 1790, of Shakespeare's autograph, "from a deed in Mr. Wallis's hand belonging to the Featherstonhaugh family" This is the one on the deed of 1613, now belonging to the City of London.

301—314. Fourteen sketches, taken by Blight, in 1863, of objects in the interior and on the exterior of Stratford Church.

315—319. Five original sketches, taken by Blight in 1865, illustrative of the journeys of Shakespeare, viz., Stratton Audley, Grendon Underwood and Aylesbury.

320. Stratford Church. Drawn by R. B. Wheler. Engraved by F. Eginton, Birm. 1806.

321—330. Sketches by Blight, very carefully executed, of the curious ancient misereres in Stratford Church.

331. Windsor Castle and part of the town, copied from a painting, executed about the year 1690, preserved at Greenwich Hospital.

332—337. Sketches taken by Blight in 1863 of Exhall, Wixford, Temple Grafton, Marston, Barton, and the back of the Falcon Inn at Bidford.

338. A very old house near the Three Pigeons at Brentford, sketched by Blight in 1866.

339. An old wooden bridge that was formerly between Windsor and Eton, a copy made in 1863 from an early painting in the possession of G. Tuck, esq., of Windsor.

340. Old timbered house near Datchet, 1863.

341—361. Original sketches, taken by Blight in 1863, 1864 and 1865, illustrative of Shakespeare's Journeys, viz., Warwick, Wixford, Hillborough, Broom, Marston, Eton, Barton-on-the-Heath, Bidford, Pebworth, Beaconsfield, Temple Grafton, Waddesdon, Pershore and Grendon Underwood

362. Interior of an old Inn at Rochester; Ruins of the Pharos at Dover. Two sketches by F. W. Fairholt.

363. St. Christopher, one of the hoodmould terminations of the doorway leading from the Chancel into the Charnel House in Stratford Church, 1864.

364. A ground-plan of the Charnel House in Stratford Church, copied from a drawing made by R. B. Wheler.

365. 366. Old timbered houses at Datchet, 1863.

367. Elizabethan Gateway, St. Alban's, 1867.

368—370. Three sketches by Blight of objects in Stratford Church, one being the Chancel doorway leading to the Charnel House, taken in 1863.

371. Elizabethan house at Rochester, 1863.

372. Old timbered house at Tetsworth, 1864.

373. Shakespeare's Crab-tree, a woodcut from Ireland's Picturesque Views on the Avon, 1795.

374. A curious example of mosaic pavement on the altar steps of Stratford Church, from a drawing by R. B. Wheler.

375. A cornice, &c., in Stratford Church, sketched by Blight.

376. Ancient window in the cellar at the Crown Inn, Rochester, sketched by Blight in 1863.

377. The entrance to Stratford Church. *Blight.*

378. The ancient stocks at Windsor Castle, a sketch taken by F. W. Fairholt in 1847.

379—381. Plans of Dover, Rochester and Canterbury, of foreign execution, c. 1650.

382. A pen-and-ink sketch of the bronze door handle on the door of Stratford Church, a work of art of the fifteenth century.

383—386. Four water-colour drawings by J. C. Buckler, 1823, two of the exterior and two of the interior of Stratford Church.

387—389. Three interesting etchings of Dover, the work of W. Hollar, 1643.

390. Windsor Castle and the Little Park, a foreign engraving of the early part of the seventeenth century.

391—396. Original sketches by Blight of small objects in Stratford Church and at Wixford, taken in 1863.

397. Armes in the windowes of the Church, Stratford-super-Avon. From Dugdale, 1656.

398. Engraved portrait of Dr. Caius, 1561.

399. A large general view of Stratford-on-Avon taken by Blight, in August, 1863, from the Hill.

400. An unfinished sketch of the Wier Brake. Blight, 1864.

401—403. Sketches of Henley Street and the Bridge, copied from old views.

404. 405. Two water-colour drawings of the Mill Bridge, ait and river, executed by Blight in 1864.

406. The kitchen and chimney corner at the Birth-Place, from a sketch taken by F. W. Fairholt on August the 29th, 1839.

407—412. Six original sketches, taken by Blight in 1864, of portions of the Birth-Place.

413. The back of Mr. Hunt's house in Church Street, as it is believed to have been when possessed by the Cloptons.

414. The end of the Birth-Place. Blight, 1864.

415. The Mill-bridge at Stratford. Blight, 1863.

416. Panelling in the Attic at the Birth-Place, sketched by Blight in 1864.

417. The Room in which Shakespeare was born, from a sketch taken by Fairholt in 1839.

418. Old doorway at Anne Hathaway's Cottage, a sketch taken by Blight in 1864.

419. The Shop at the Birth-Place, an interior looking to street, from a sketch by Fairholt.

420. The bacon cupboard at Anne Hathaway's Cottage, 1697, sketched by Blight in 1864.

421. The Shop at the Birth-Place, an interior looking towards kitchen. From the sketch made by Fairholt for his Home of Shakspere.

422—424. Three large views of the Mill-bridge at Stratford, taken by Blight from different positions in 1864.

425. The Wier-Brake, Stratford-on-Avon. Blight, 1864.

426. Interior of Anne Hathaway's Cottage, Blight, 1863.

427. A grate, in the possession of Mrs. James, brought from the Birth-Place. Sketched by Blight in 1864.

428. Elizabethan houses at Henley-in-Arden, a very pretty sketch taken by Blight in the year 1864.

429. A room in Anne Hathaway's Cottage. Blight, 1864.

430. The Great Hall at Charlecote, as described by Washington Irving, from a sketch made by Fairholt before the alterations.

431. Charlecote House and Park. Drawn by I. D. Harding. Engraved by W. Radclyffe. Birmingham, published by the Proprietors, March 27th, 1827.

432. An unfinished view of Stratford-on-Avon, taken from the Cross-on-the-Hill, c. 1827.

433. An elaborate view of the front exterior of Charlecote House, taken about the year 1770, and believed to be the work of one Rogers, a Birmingham drawing-master.

434. A room on the right-hand of the entrance to Anne Hathaway's Cottage, a sketch taken by Blight in 1864.

435. 436. The room behind the shop at the Birth Place; the entrance to the chimney in the room in that building now used for the Museum. Two large sketches by Blight, 1864.

437. The interior of the old panelled room at Abingdon Abbey, the residence of Shakespeare's grand-daughter. Sketched by Blight in 1863.

438. Old settle at Anne Hathaway's Cottage, from a sketch by F. W. Fairholt.

439. The Market-cross and High Street, Stratford-on-Avon, from a drawing made by C. F. Green in 1821.

440. Ancient Houses, Southwark. Taylor, 1883.

441. The Market-Cross, with the timbered corners of Wood Street and Henley Street, Stratford-on-Avon, from a drawing by C. F. Green, 1821.

442. The interior of the College Hall, Stratford-on-Avon, copied from a drawing made by Jordan about the year 1790.

443. The tomb of Sir Thomas Lucy in Charlecote Church, an elaborate sketch made by Blight in 1863.

444. The Shakespeare Inn, Shottery, in its old timbered state, a copy of a sketch made by Fairholt in 1847.

445. The Elizabethan carved oak bedstead at Anne Hathaway's Cottage, a sketch taken by Fairholt in 1863.

446. The Birth-Place Museum. Blight, 1863.

447—448. Shottery and Wilmecote, copies of sketches made for me by Fairholt in 1852.

449. Henley-in-Arden. Blight, 1864.

450—454. The Grammar-School, Stratford-on-Avon. Five sketches, consisting of two original ones by Blight, and three others copied by him from drawings by Fairholt.

455. A Plan of Stratford-on-Avon, executed by Samuel Winter about the year 1760.

> Only two original plans of Stratford by Winter, the earliest scientific local surveyor, are known to exist, viz., the present one (from the Greene collection) and another in the Birth-Place Library. My copy is clearly by some years the earliest, as it has fewer houses than are noted in the other.

456. The western side of the Birth-Place. Blight, 1864.

457—462. Six large sketches of portions of the Birth-Place. Blight, 1864.

463. A general view of Stratford-on-Avon showing the Bancroft, a copy of a drawing made by R. B. Wheler about the year 1800.

464—467. Four sketches of portions of the Birth-Place, taken by Blight in 1864.

468. The Mill-bridge, Stratford. Blight, 1864.

469. The Grammar-School, Stratford. A view of the exterior, in Church Street, taken by Blight in 1864.

470. Small Elizabethan carved oak chair, formerly in the Birth-Place. Sketched by Blight, 1864. This has been positively exhibited as the identical chair in which the boy Shakespeare was accustomed to sit.

471. The Stratford School, interior. Sketched by Blight in 1863.

472. An upper room at the Birth-Place. Sketched by Blight in 1863.

473. A water-colour drawing of the attic at the Birth-Place, sketched by Blight in 1864.

474. Whitehall and Lambeth.   Hollar, c. 1650.

475. 476. Two large drawings of upper rooms in Anne Hathaway's Cottage, sketched by Blight in 1864.

477. Interior of Anne Hathaway's Cottage, drawn and etched by W. Rider. Published November 1st., 1827, by the Artist and by J. Merridew, Leamington and Warwick.

478. The westernmost lower room at the Birth-Place, sketched by Blight in August, 1864.

479. The Guild - pits, Stratford - on - Avon. Blight, 1862.

480. The back of the Birth-place, c. 1850.

481. A view of the Church and Avon Bank house, taken by R. B. Wheler from the Old Town in 1800.   A copy.

482. A view of the Birth-Place as it appeared when the contiguous buildings were first removed.

483—499. Seventeen views of St. Paul's Cathedral, drawn and engraved by Hollar in 1656, 1657, and 1658.

500. The Birth-Place, c. 1849. A copy.

501. A view of London, rare and useless. Sebastianus Cipriani arch. inuent. et delin. Alexander Speculus sculp.

502 A sketch of the bass-relief of David and Goliah formerly at the Birth-Place, taken by Blight in 1864.

503 An elaborate sketch of the Elizabethan house in the High Street, Stratford, taken by Blight in 1864.

504. The Market-Cross and surrounding houses at the time of the Jubilee in 1769. This is a modern coloured lithograph, and is not, I believe, reliable.

505. A large coloured sketch by Blight, executed in 1864, of one of the attics in Anne Hathaway's Cottage.

506. A water-colour drawing of the Clopton Bridge, Stratford-on-Avon, by Rogers, a Birmingham schoolmaster, c. 1762.

507. 508. A tower of Charlecote House ; and a copy of a representation of the house from an old painting in the hall.

509. The lower steps of the stairs at the Birth-Place, sketched by Blight in 1864.

510 Interior of the Hall of the Middle Temple, where Twelfth Night was performed in 1602, sketched by Blight in 1867. See No. 515.

511. The old gateway, Charlecote. Blight, 1863.

512. Bearley Church, from a drawing c. 1810.

513. Bishopton Chapel, from a drawing c. 1800.

514. A cornice of figure heads in the Elizabethan house in the High Street, Stratford-on-Avon, sketched by Blight in 1864.

515. An elaborate coloured view of the screen and roof of the Hall in the Middle Temple, executed by Blight in 1867. See No. 510.

516. The cornice of the Elizabethan house in the High Street, Stratford-on-Avon, that in which the date of 1596 is recorded. Blight, 1864.

517. A copy of an old sketch in water-colours formerly preserved in the Daniel library, and described as an "original drawing of the Stratford Jubilee, 1769," but it is evidently of a later date, executed probably about the year 1800.

518. A sketch taken by Blight, in 1864, of a lock (in the possession of Mrs. James) brought from the Birth-Place.

519. A carved oak chest at Mrs. James's, said to have formerly been in Anne Hathaway's Cottage. A sketch by Blight, taken in 1864.

520. An old room at Anne Hathaway's Cottage, with an ancient stone bench. Sketched by Blight in 1864.

521—523. Three sketches by Blight of the interior of the Birth-Place, including one of the Birth-Room, 1864.

524. An upper room at Anne Hathaway's Cottage, 1864.

525. The eastern portion of the room behind the shop at the Birth-Place, sketched by Blight in 1864.

526. William Shakspeare, engraved by C. Picart from the original Print by Martin Droeshout. Published April 23rd, 1827, by A. Wivell.

527. The shop at the Birth-Place. Blight, 1864.

528. Elizabethan House, Uxbridge. Blight, 1864.

529. Interior of Stratford Church. T. G. Flowers, Edin.

530. The Nag's Head Inn, Bicester. Sketched by Blight in 1865.

531. Scroll-work in Stratford Church. Sketched by Blight in 1864.

532. Elizabethan house at Bristol, an elaborate pen-and-ink sketch by F. W. Fairholt, c. 1847.

533. Stratford-upon-Avon Church. The western end. Fahee lithog. Published by J. Ward.

534—543. Birth-place sketches by Blight, including copies of drawings of the northern exteriors before the restoration, assumed relics of bedstead, portions of the interior, and desks absurdly stated to have belonged to the poet.

544. A long view of London, showing the Globe and other old theatres, with views of the exterior and interior of St. Paul's Cathedral. D. King delin. et excudit, anno 1658. This engraving is evidently of copies of earlier drawings.

545. Braun's view of London, 1574. Coloured.

With minute variations from the copy, No. 28.

546. A View of London about the year 1560, done from a print engraven on wood in Sir Hans Sloane's collection, and copyed in small, 1738.

547 Elevation of the Birth-Place as restored.

548. Plan of the Birth-Place before the restoration, showing the timbers of the original first floor.

549. A full-sized plan of the ancient wrought-iron fastening to the Birth-Room window.

550. A ground-plan of the Birth-Place, taken shortly before the restoration.

551. A copy of a view of the exterior of the Birth-Place, taken by John Sharp c. 1790.

552. Somerset House in its Original State, with the various Buildings on the Banks of the River Thames as far as Westminster, from an antient Painting at Dulwich College. Published by Herbert and Wilkinson, 1809.

553. A Map or Ground Plot of the Citty of London and the Suburbes thereof, that is to say, all which is within the Iurisdic-

tion of the Lord Mayor or properlie calldt London, by which is exactly demonstrated the present condition thereof since the last sad accident of fire, the blanke space signifeing the burnt part, and where the houses are exprest, those places yet standing. Sould by Iohn Overton at the White Horse in Little Brittaine, next doore to little S. Bartholomew gate, 1666.

554. A long view of London engraved abroad about the year 1640, with forty-three references to numbers. The Swan, the Bear Garden, and the Globe Theatre are in the fore-ground.

555. Londen. A foreign view, 1623.

556. A View of London from Howel's Londinopolis, 1657, with forty-six references to numbers. It is a copy of some earlier drawing, the Globe and other theatres being shown.

557. A Portrait of James the First on horseback, with a view of London beneath, 1621. One theatre shown.

558. 559. Hollar's two long Views of London, 1666, both restricted to the north of the river.

560. The Temple and its gardens, 1720.

561. Three Views of Kenilworth Castle, 1656.

562. Sketches, with details, of the ancient Cross at Henley-in-Arden, c. 1810.

563. A rough ground-plan of the College at Stratford-on-Avon, with the adjoining roads, made very early in the sixteenth century. The site of the *tyth barne* is shown. This plan, by far the earliest of any part of Stratford known to exist, is on vellum, and originally formed one side of the cover of an old manuscript volume of local collections.

564. 565. Two Views of Windsor Castle and Park, one c. 1740, the other published in 1775 from a drawing by Sir Peter Lely.

566. 567. London and Westminster, two views; Ioannes Norden Anglus descripsit, 1593.

568. 569. Later copies, "augmented" by Speed, 1610, of the two last views, that of London showing two theatres in Southwark.

570—572. Paintings on the north side of the Chancel of the Guild Chapel, viz., the combat of Heraclius with the son of Cordroy; the decapitation of Cordroy, King of Persia, by Heraclius; the miracles of the Holy Cross; and the Invention of the Holy Cross. The original drawings made by Fisher in 1804.

573—576. Other original drawings by Fisher of the paintings on the walls of the Guild Chapel, viz., the Exaltation of the Holy Cross; St. George and the Dragon; the Death of Thomas à Becket; and the Judgment of the Whore of Babylon.

577. Figures on the Porch of the Guild Chapel; arms on the spandrils of the north door, and carved work on the spandrils of the south door. Original drawings by Fisher, 1804. These do not appear to have been engraved.

578. 579. Coloured Views of the Birth-Room and the exterior of the Birth-Place, taken in 1856, before the restoration. Fred. Dangerfield, chromo-lith.

580. A large view of the exterior of the Birth-Place, from a sketch taken in 1846. Drawn by J. T. Clark. Engraved by T. H. Ellis.

581. Another large view of the Birth-Place, published in the Shakspere Newspaper, 1847. E. Wild sc.

582. Exterior of Anne Hathaway's Cottage, a small flock of sheep and a dog in the foreground. C. Graf lith., London. Published by F. and E. Ward.

583. A view of the Birth-Place, c. 1835. Drawn, Printed and Published by G. Rowe, artist, &c., Exeter Hall, Cheltenham.

584. The West Prospect of the Church of St. Ethelburgh, with some of the Elizabethan houses of old London. R. West delin., 1736. W. H. Toms sculpsit.

585. Shakespeare's Birth-Room. E. T. Parris, 1864.

586. Interior Views of Grammar School-rooms in which Shakespeare was educated, from original sketches by H. B. Clements.

587. Exterior of the Birth-Place. C. Graf lith. Published by F. and E. Ward.

588. A large view of the exterior of the Birth-Place, "engraved by Alfred Baker, aged 13 years, from a sketch taken in 1804."

London, Published for Alfred Baker by Colnaghi and Co., Cockspur street.

589. The South Prospect of the Church of St. Saviour in Southwark.   R. West delin., 1737.   W. H. Toms sculp.   Published March 18, 1739.

590. 591. Stratford Church, the River and the Mill Bridge, copies of paintings executed about the year 1710.

592. A View of London, taken in or before the year 1613, showing the old Globe Theatre. Published by Holland in 1620.

593. The House in which Shakespeare was born.   Drawn by Mrs. P. Dighton, and published 1835.   Uncoloured.

594. A plan of commercial designs on the eastern side of the river at Stratford-on-Avon, as projected by Andrew Yarranton, 1677.

595. A large water-colour drawing, by Blight, of the back of the Grammar School and the old buildings in that locality.   1864.

596. The room in which Shakespeare was born, drawn by Mrs. P. Dighton, and published 1835.   Uncoloured.

597. Ruins at Kenilworth. Ireland, 1795.

598. Bidford Grange. Ireland, 1795.

599. Interior of Ann Hathaway's House. Drawn by Mrs. P. Dighton, and published 1835. Uncoloured.

600. Charlecote Great Hall. In lithotint by F. W. Hulme. From a sketch by J. G. Jackson. Published by Chapman and Hall, London, Sept. 1st, 1845.

601. Shakespeare reclining on the banks of the Avon, with Stratford Church in the distance. Ireland, 1795.

602. Bidford and its Bridge. Ireland, 1795.

603. Exterior of Charlcote House. In lithotint by F. W. Hulme. From a sketch by J. G. Jackson. Published by Chapman and Hall, London, Sept. 1st, 1845.

604. The Market-Cross, Stratford-on-Avon, with the Elizabethan houses in Wood Street, as they appeared in 1820. Drawn and lithographed by C. F. Green.

605. Effigy of Sir Thomas Lucy. Ireland, 1795.

606. The Avon, the Bancroft and the Jubilee Amphitheatre of 1769. Ireland, 1795.

607. The house in which Shakespeare was born. Drawn by Mrs. P. Dighton, and published in 1835. This is a coloured copy of No. 593.

608. The Room in which Shakespeare was born. Drawn by Mrs. P. Dighton, and published in 1835. This is a coloured copy of No. 596.

609. Effigy of John Combe. Ireland, 1795.

610. House at Shotery in which Ann Hathaway, the wife of Shakspere, resided. Ireland, 1795.

611. Shakespeare's Desk at Stratford-on-Avon, still to be seen in the Grammar School where he received his education. Drawn by Mrs. P. Dighton, and published in 1835. Coloured.

612 Ann Hathaway's Bed and Chair, Drawn by Mrs. P. Dighton, and published in 1835. Uncoloured.

613. Stratford Bridge, &c. Ireland, 1795.

614. Clopton House, near Stratford-on-Avon. Ireland, 1795.

615. The House of Ann Hathaway. Drawn

by Mrs. P. Dighton, and published in 1835 as in No. 611.

616. The House at Stratford in which Shakspear was born. Exterior. At top is " Pl. xxxiv.," so it is doubtlessly from some work a reference to which I am unable to give. It is a lithograph, apparently executed about the year 1830.

617. A coloured facsimile of Norden's plan of Windsor and the Little Park, 1607.

618. The Church and Free-school, Hampton Lucy, 1823. Captain Saunders del. C. F. Green lithog., 1824. This lithograph was not published.

619. The Hall at Charlecote where Shakespeare was tried. Drawn by Mrs. P. Dighton, and published in 1835.

620. A western view of Stratford Church. A wood engraving from the Penny Magazine of Sept. 1st, 1832.

621. Herne's Oak, 1812. A very rare etching.

622. A lithograph, c. 1824, inscribed *Shakspeare's Hall*. It shows the whole of Chapel Street.

623. Shakespeare's Seal-ring. Blight, 1864.

624. A quaint early carved figure in the Crown Inn at Rochester, sketched by Blight in October, 1863.

625. Ancient bridge over Brent Brook, near Hanwell sketched by Blight in July, 1864.

626. Exterior of the Birth-Place. Drawn from Nature and on Stone by J. Brandard. Day and Haghe, lithographers to the Queen. c. 1840.

627. Shakespeare's Desk at Stratford-on-Avon. Drawn by Mrs. P. Dighton. An uncoloured copy of No. 611.

628. A plan of Norwich, xvii. Cent.

629. Inn Yard, Rochester. A pen-and-ink sketch by F. W. Fairholt, taken about the year 1847.

630. Shakespeare's Cliff, a pencil sketch by Fairholt.

631. The Room in which Shakspere was born. Drawn from Nature and on stone by J. Brandard.

632. Charlecote Hall. Drawn and Etched by W. Rider. Published Nov. 1st, 1827,

by the Artist and by J. Merriden, Leamington and Warwick. A proof.

633. The back of Charlecote Hall. Drawn from Nature and on Stone by J. Brandard. Leamington, Published by C. Elston, 12, Lower Union Parade.

634. Middle Row and Bridge Street, c. 1835; a copy by Blight of a drawing by Mrs. E. F. Flower now in the Birth-Place Museum.

635. The Kitchen in Anne Hathaway's Cottage, a copy of a sketch taken by Fairholt about the year 1847.

636. Ancient passage in Windsor Street, Stratford-on-Avon, sketch by Blight in 1864.

637. Exterior of the Birth-Place. Drawn and Etched by W. Rider. Published November 1st, 1827, by the Artist and by J. Merriden, Leamington and Warwick. A proof.

638. Exterior of the Birth-Place before the restoration. W. L. Walton, 1861. M. and H. Hanhart, lith.

639. The Room in which Shakespeare was

born. J. Brandard lith. Sold only at the Shakespeare House.

640. The Sword of State anciently borne before the Mayor of Stratford-on-Avon. Blight, 1864.

641. The Birth-Place. A coloured exterior view, with a portion of Henley Street, c. 1835.

642. Exterior of the Birth-Place. A large unfinished etching, c. 1810, showing the Swan and Maidenhead before that inn was refronted. A man leading a horse, a dog preceding him, in the foreground. Very rare, if not unique.

643 A view of the Birth-Place and Henley Street, from a photograph taken shortly before the restoration.

644. The Church at Billesley, c. 1810. A copy.

645—648. Four views of the Birth-Place before the restoration, all being copies made by Blight in 1862.

649. The Mill-Bridge, Stratford-on-Avon, and the Cross-on-the-Hill, a sketch by Blight taken in August, 1864.

650. A Prospect of Warwick, July 7th, 1725. Stukeley del.

651. David and Goliah, a design in plaster formerly in the Swan and Maidenhead. Wood-engraving, from Ireland's Views on the Avon, 1795.

652. An East Prospect of the College in Stratford, 1765. An original drawing in sepia.

653. Arms of the Merchants of the Staple in a pane of glass formerly at the Birth-Place. Ireland, 1795.

654. A view of Stratford-on-Avon from the bridge. Drawn by R. B. Wheler. Engraved by F. Eginton, Birm. 1806.

655—657. Stratford-on-Avon College, the Bridge, and the Jubilee Amphitheatre. R. B. Wheler, 1806.

658. A House in Stratford-upon-Avon in which the famous poet Shakespear was born. R. Greene delin., B. Cole sculpsit. From the Gentleman's Magazine, July, 1769.

659. A view of Stratford-on-Avon, 1830.

660. Old Houses at Charlecote. Blight, 1863.

661. A view of the inner ground-floor room at the Birth-Place, a wood-engraving from the Shakspere Newspaper, 1847.

662. Sketch of an ancient miserere in which a mermaid is represented, now in the Birth-Place Museum, and said to have been formerly in the Guild Chapel. I doubt this, and should be much obliged if any one would supply me with information respecting its history.

663. Bushwood Hall, Sydney Davenport's, 1825.

664—665. Old timbered houses on the Water-Side. Blight, 1863.

666. Henley Street and the Swan Inn, near the Birth-Place, a drawing made by Jordan about the year 1785.

667. Backs of old timbered houses in Ely Street, Stratford-on-Avon, a sketch taken by Blight in September, 1863.

668. Old timbered house at Charlecote. Sketched by Blight in 1863.

669—670. Two sketches of the open fields at Crimscote, taken by Blight in 1863.

671. The House in Stratford-upon-Avon in which Shakespear was born. Ph. de la

Motte, 1788. A modern impression from the original plate.

672. A water-colour drawing of the exterior of Anne Hathaway's Cottage, taken about the year 1830. Artist's name unknown.

673. Exterior of the Birth-Place. Drawn by R. B. Wheler. Engraved by F. Eginton, Birm. 1806.

674. Ancient well at Shottery. Blight, 1863.

675. Corner-top of old house at Henley-in-Arden. Fairholt, 1846.

676. Figures on the Hathaway bedstead. Blight, 1863.

677. Ancient lock on the Tower door of the Guild Chapel. Blight, 1864.

678—679. Two sketches of wooden figures formerly in the roof of the Guild Chapel. Blight, 1864.

680—681. The Shop of Shakspeare's Birth-Place, C. F. Green lithog., March, 1823. —Kitchen of the Birth-place of Shakspeare, C. F. Green delin. et lithog., clearly executed at or about the same time as the last.

682—685. Four sketches of objects at the Guild Chapel, taken by Blight in 1864.

686. The Interior of an old English theatre, Sir John Falstaff and Mrs Quickly in the foreground, from Kirkman's Wits or Sport upon Sport, 1672. This is the very rare original engraving, not the later copy so often substituted for it.

687. An ancient door at the back of the house in the Old Town, the one believed to have been tenanted by Shakespeare's son-in-law, John Hall. Blight, 1864.

688. The Lich-gate at Welford. Fairholt, 1846.

689. Shakespeare's School and Old Guildhall, Stratford-on-Avon. London, J. Harwood, 1847.

690—697. Sketches, taken by Blight in 1863, 1864 and 1865, of objects in Stratford-on-Avon, Charlecote and Shottery, including some at the Guild Chapel and the Birth-Place.

698. Interior of Gray's Inn Hall, 1804. The Comedy of Errors was performed there in 1594.

699. Arms of the Merchants of the Staple.—

The Old Sign affixed to Shakspeare's House. C. F. Green, lithog. 1824.

700. The Birth-Place, a copy of an old drawing.

701—702. Tower Arch, Guild Chapel, and a mullion and sill in the nave window. Blight, 1864.

703—706. Paintings in the Guild Chapel, outline pencil drawings by R. B. Wheler.

704. The old font, Bishopton. Blight, 1867.

705. A facsimile of the inscription on the gravestone of Shakespeare, published by Ward, in 1827.

706. See No. 703.

707. Ancient door at Weston Church. Fairholt, 1846.

708. A south-east view of Bishopton Chapel, an original drawing in sepia by Richard Greene, c. 1762.

709. Charlecote Church, an original sketch in sepia by J. J. Jackson, 1845.

710. Baynard's Castle, from a view of old London painted by Claude de Jongh in the year 1650.

711. The Charnel House, Stratford-on-Avon, from a drawing made by R. B. Wheler, c. 1810.

712. Atherston upon Stour in Warwickshire, an original drawing by Richard Greene, c. 1762.

713. A view of London from Tootehill Fields Hollar, 1641.

714—720. Sketches of objects in the Birth-Place of Guild Chapel, taken by Blight in 1864.

721. Ancient carved house at Tewkesbury. Fairholt, 1846.

722. Appearance of Shakspeare's Birth-Place in 1824. C. F. Green, delin. et lithog.

723—726. Sketches of objects at the Birth-Place and Guild Chapel, taken by Blight in 1864.

727. The font and piscina at Bishopton Chapel, from a drawing made by R. B. Wheler.

728. Weston Church, co. Warwick. A sketch by Fairholt, 1846.

729. Exterior of the Birth-Place. Drawn and engraved by J. Storer. Published in the year 1818.

F

730. The House at Stratford in which Shakspere lived. A Smith sculp. London, printed for J. Bell, 1786.

731. A south-west view of Alveston Church near Stratford-on-Avon, an original drawing by Richard Greene, c. 1762.

732. The Chapel at Bishopton, an original drawing, c. 1810.

733. The basement wall of Nash's House, Stratford-on-Avon, sketched by Blight in 1865.

734. A long narrow view of London showing the old theatres. By some foreign artist, c. 1640.

735. A view of London, showing, in the foreground, the first Globe Theatre, the one in which many of Shakespeare's masterpieces were originally produced. It was engraved by Hondius in 1610, and published in 1611.

736. A view of London from the river. Hollar, c. 1650.

737. The Clyff of Dover from Sea. By Hollar, c. 1644. This and No. 193 are the earliest views of Shakespeare's Cliff known to exist.

738. A minute sketch of an old theatre in the engraved title-page of the Tragedy of Messalina by N. Richards; London, printed for Dan. Frere, 1640.

739. A piece of carved wood in the Birth-Place Museum, said to have been formerly part of a doorway at the Guild Chapel. A sketch by Blight, 1865.

740—741. Views of Richmond and Nonsuch.

742. Shakespeare's Courting-Chair! An engraving from Ireland's Views, 1795.

743. The silver paten, Bishopton Chapel, 1571. Blight, 1867.

744. The Mill-Bridge, Stratford-on-Avon, when in process of demolition. From a photograph taken in 1867.

745. Shakspeare's Birth-Place as it appeared previous to 1769. Published by Henry Merriden, Coventry.

746. South Part of the Chamber in which Shakspeare was born. C. F. Green, delin. et lithog. 1824.

747. Shakespeare's House at Stratford-on-Avon. J. Boosey and Co., lithog. 310, Strand.

748. House in High Street, Stratford-on-Avon, 1829, A pen-and-ink drawing by Captain Saunders.

749. Henley Street, Stratford-on-Avon, a copy of a sketch by Captain Saunders. This view shows the corner of the old timbered workhouse.

750. Silver chalice, Bishopton. Blight, 1867.

751. Ancient silver paten in the Church of Clifford-Chambers.

752. Shakspeare's House as it appeared in 1787.—Shakespeare's House as it now appears, 1837. Woodcuts from the Casket of April the 23rd, 1837.

753. The House in which Shakspeare was born. J. Archer del., W. Finden sc.

754. Exterior of the Birth-Place. Engraving of the house and inn, as they appeared, about the year 1810. Poultry in the foreground. The letter S conspicuously seen in a compartment over the window of the butcher's shop.

755. Ancient door in the house in the Old Town mentioned in No. 687. Sketched by Blight, 1864.

756. North-west view of Stratford College, 1808.

757. A diminute map of Warwickshire, 1643.

758. Oval view of Stratford-on-Avon, c. 1720, a pencil copy from an old painting.

759. Moll Cutpurse,—Mistress Mall. The original engraving.

760. Charlecote Church, a copy from Saunders.

761. Old timbered house in the Rother Market. Blight, 1864.

762. A piece of wood-carving in the Birth-Place Museum, said to have formerly been in the College. Sketched by Blight in 1865.

763. Bishopton Chapel, Warwickshire, N.E.

764. Houses in Henley Street, including the Birth-Place. W. Alexander del., 1820.

765. Exterior of the Birth-Place. A view of the front taken from the west in October, 1792, giving the old timbered appearance of the whole. A wood-engraving from Ireland's Views, 1795.

766. A small view of the Birth-Place, copied from Saunders' illustrations to Washington Irving's paper on Stratford-on-Avon.

767. Figures from the Guild Chapel, sketches copied by Blight from drawings by R B. Wheler.

768. A very curious litttle view of an old English theatre, the engraved title-page of the tragedy of Roxana, 1632.

769. Figures formerly at Stratford College, sketches copied by Blight from drawings by R. B. Wheler.

770. Arms in the Windows of the Guild Chapel; armes cut in stone on the Front of the Porch. Dugdale, 1656.

771. The Market-Cross, from a drawing by Captain Saunders.

772. Daisy Hill, a farmhouse, anciently the keeper's lodge, where Shakespeare is mendaciously said to have been imprisoned. A woodcut from Ireland's Views, 1795.

773. A view of the Birth-Place and the Swan and Maidenhead, from a drawing taken about the year 1810. The landlord just coming out of the Swan. Three posts in the foreground. A wood-engraving, Sears sc.

774. Exterior of the Birth-Place, a wood-engraving from the Monthly Magazine, February, 1818.

775. Charlecote Vicarage. An old timbered house. Drawn by P. Dewint. Engraved by W. Radclyffe, Birmingham. Published by the Proprietors, Oct. 1st. 1823. Printed by W. and T. Radclyffe.

776. The back of Anne Hathaway's Cottage, from a sketch by F. W. Fairholt, c. 1847.

777. The Birth-Place, 1847. W. J. Linton sc.

778. Alveston Church and old timbered house, 1837. Sketched from Nature and on Stone by Mrs. Bracebridge. Day and Haghe, lithographers to the King.

779. Anne Hathaway's Cottage, from a sketch taken by F. W. Fairholt in 1847.

780. Interior of Hathaway's Cottage, Shottery. Drawn and Etched by W. Rider. Published November 1st, 1827, by the Artist and by J. Merriden, Leamington and Warwick.

781. Kitchen of the House in which Shakspere was born. Etch'd by S. Ireland. Published in 1795.

782. The Birth-Place, a sketch " taken during the last grand festival." London, Published by N. Whittock, No. 39, Rathbone Place.

783. The Effigy of the Earl of Totness, from the original in Stratford Church.

784. The Monumental Effigy and Grave-stone. Ireland, 1795.

785. Shakspere's House, New Place, Guild Chapel and Grammar School. Sam. Ireland del. 1795.

786. David and Goliah, from the plaster relievo formerly in the House of Shakspeare's birth. C. F. Green lithog. 1824.

787. The Church and Free-School, Hampton Lucy. Captain Saunders del. C. F. Green lithog. c. 1822. This lithograph varies from that of No.

788. Charlecote Park, the Seat of George Lucy, esq., with the house in the distance. Drawn and Engraved by T. Radclyffe. Published by W. Emans, August 15th, 1829, Bromsgrove Street, Birmingham.

789. The Keeper's Lodge, Fulbroke Park.

Drawn and Etched by W. Rider. Published November 1st, 1827, by the Artist and by J. Merriden, Leamington and Warwick. A proof.

790. Interior of the Middle Temple Hall. Published May 15, 1804, by Vernor and Hood.

791—794. Copies by Blight of sketches of the interior of Aston Cantlow Church, old house at Wilmecote and Bishopton Chapel.

795—842. A series of sketches by Blight, chiefly original but including a few copies, of objects at Shottery, Stratford-on-Avon, Wilmecote, Hampton Lucy, the Dingles, Snitterfield, Bearley, Aston Cantlowe and Luddington.

843. The Attic at the Birth-Place. F. W. Fairholt, 1847.

844—849. Original sketches by Blight of of objects at Stratford-on-Avon, taken in 1863 and 1864.

850. Exterior of the Birth-Place, July 30th, 1848, a copy by Blight of a sketch by F. Goodall, A.R.A.

851. A view of Aston Cantlowe, taken by Blight, 1863.

852. An original drawing of the exterior of the Birth-Place, executed by Richard Greene between the years 1762 and 1769. This is the earliest representation of the Birth-Place known to exist.

853. 854. Charlecote and Daisy Hill, copies by Blight of sketches by Captain Saunders.

855—858. Sketches made by Blight in 1864 of objects at Stratford-on-Avon.

859. 860. Westminster and the river. W. Hollar fecit, 1647.

861. Interior of the Council Chamber, Stratford-on-Avon.

862. Two pencil views of Bishopton Chapel, c. 1810.

863. A view of the Rother Market, c. 1780, copied from a drawing by Jordan.

864. Elizabethan houses in Wood Street, copied from a sketch taken by Mrs E. F. Flower, c. 1835.

865. The painted maypole at Welford. Fairholt, 1855.

866. Stratford Church, River and Mill, from a painting executed about the year 1720.

867. Henley Street and the old timbered workhouse, from a sketch taken by Mrs. E. F. Flower, c. 1835.

868. Snitterfield Church, from a drawing by Fairholt.

869. Snitterfield Church, S. E. Allan E. Everitt del. J. Brandard lith. Published by H. T. Cooke, Warwick.

870. The back of Charlecote House. From Ireland's Views, 1795.

871. The western end of the Guild Chapel, a pretty sketch taken by Blight in 1863.

872. The Elizabethan House in the High Street, Stratford-on-Avon. F. W. Fairholt del. C. D. Laing sc.

873. Portrait of Florio, 1611. Gul. Hole sculp.

874. A carved wooden impost at the New Inn, Gloucester. A sketch taken in 1846.

875. A view of the ancient cross and old houses

at Henley-in-Arden, a sketch by F. W. Fairholt taken in 1846.

876. The stair-case at the Birth-Place. A sketch by Blight, 1864.

877. Exterior of the Birth-Place. Part of the Swan and Maidenhead, all the cottages on the left and a small portion of the White Lion Inn shown. An original water-colour drawing by Shepherd.

878. S. Marie Ouer's in Southwarke A large etching of this interesting Church. W. Hollar fecit. 1647.

879. Exterior of the Middle Temple Hall, 1803.

880—893. Sketches by Blight, taken in 1863, 1866, and 1867, of objects at Shottery, Stratford-on-Avon, Marsh Gibbon, Milcote, Barcheston, Clifford, Bearley, Barton-on-the-Heath, Welford and Grendon Underwood.

894. A pencil sketch of the Combe monument in Stratford Church, c. 1820. The artist's name unknown.

895. Exterior of the Birth-Place and part of Henley Street. London, J. Harwood, 26, Fenchurch St., Nov. 1st, 1847.

896. The back of the Shakespeare Tavern, Shottery, July, 1848, from a sketch by F. Goodall, A.R.A.

897—909. Sketches, chiefly original, made by Blight in 1863, 1864 and 1865, of objects at Stratford-on-Avon, Shottery and Charlecote.

910. The Birth-Place and the Swan. H. Fitzook del.

911. A room in Anne Hathaway's Cottage 1847. W. J. Linton sc.

912. 913. The Charnel House, Stratford-on-Avon, exterior and interior, from sketches by Captain Saunders.

914. 915. Old timbered houses at Bewdley. Blight, 1867.

916. Elizabethan room in the Old Town. Blight, 1864.

917. Shottery from the Evesham Road. Blight, 1863.

918. Old timbered school-house at Snitterfield, sketched by Captain Saunders, 1825.

919. The West View of Welcombe Hills. Published 1st Sept., 1777, by S. Hooper.

920. The shop at the Birth-Place, from a drawing by Saunders.

921. An old timbered house adjoining the workhouse in Henley Street. Blight, 1863.

922. The mud-wall of an old barn near the Thatch Tavern, sketched by Blight in the year 1864.

923. The Birth-room, from a sketch by Saunders.

924—934. Sketches by Blight, chiefly original, taken in 1863, 1864 and 1865, of objects at Stratford-on-Avon, Grendon Underwood, Charlecote and Bishopton.

935. The Indian in his boat, the one brought over to England about the year 1580, and afterwards embalmed. Supposed to be alluded to in the Tempest. A contemporary German engraving of very great rarity.

936. Pathlow Hill Farm-house, near Stratford-on-Avon, an old timbered building, sketched by Blight in 1864.

937. Elizabethan interior in the Old Town. Blight, 1864.

938. Old houses at Ipswich. Fairholt, 1847.

939. An ancient box formerly at the Birth-place. Blight, 1868.

940. The Brook - House, Stratford-on-Avon. J. Jordan del. 1799.

941. Ancient door at a house in the Old Town.

942. Exterior of the Birth-Place. A wood-engraving by Whimper.

943—951. Sketches by Blight, taken in 1862, 1865 and 1867, of objects at Stratford-on-Avon, Oxford, Charlecote and London.

952—954. Old timbered houses at Tewkesbury. Fairholt, 1846.

955. An ancient wooden pillar from the house on the north of the Churchyard, Stratford-on-Avon. Blight, 1866.

956. Elizabethan house at Gloucester. Fairholt, 1846.

957. A small room in Anne Hathaway's Cottage. Blight, 1864.

958. An Elizabethan interior, Gloucester. Fairholt, 1846.

959. A South East Prospect of Stratford-upon-Avon, 1746. R. Greene del.

960—971. Sketches by Blight, chiefly originals, taken in 1863, 1864, 1865 and 1868, of objects at Bishopton. Snitterfield, Aston Cantlowe, Welford, Shottery and Stratford-on-Avon.

972. The Church-Porch at Welford, near Stratford-on-Avon. A pen-and-ink sketch by Fairholt, taken in 1847.

973. Long Lane, near Stratford-on-Avon. Blight, 1868.

974. Old houses at Clifford Chambers. Sketched by Blight, 1863.

975—978. Sketches by Blight, taken in 1863 and 1865, of objects at Shottery, Stratford-on-Avon, Weston-on-Avon and Wilmecote.

979. The Right Honourable and most noble Henry Wriothsley, Earle of Southampton, Baron of Titchfield, Knight of the most noble Order of the Garter. Simon Passæus sculp., 1617; are to be sould in Popes Head Ally by John Sudbury and Georg Humble. A beautiful impression of this very rare engraving.

980. Shakspeare's Birth-Place as it appeared previous to the Jubilee in 1769. C. F. Green lithog., 1823.

981. North Part of the Chamber in which Shakspeare was born. C. F. Green delin. et lithog. 1824.

982. Shakspeare's Desk. Rev. R. Nixon, F.S.A., del., 1824. Fahee lithog. Printed by C. Hullmandel. Published by J. Ward.

983. The Birth-Place, c. 1800. A copy.

984. Old houses in Church Street. Sketched by Blight, 1863.

985. 986. Two views of Charlecote House, taken on August the 22nd, 1823. Artist's name unknown.

987. The old Thatch Tavern, Greenhill Street. Blight, 1863.

988. Cottages at Snitterfield. Blight, 1863.

989. Old houses in Chapel Street, Stratford-on-Avon. Blight, 1862.

990. Appearance of Shakspeare's Birth-Place in 1806. R. B. Wheler delin. C. F. Green lithog., May, 1823.

991. The Old Black Swan Inn, Stratford-on-Avon. Blight, 1863.

992. Old houses in Greenhill Street, Stratford-on-Avon. Blight, 1863.

993. Curious Elizabethan timbered house at Tiddington, near Stratford-on-Avon, sketched by Blight in 1863.

994. The roof of the chapel in the Manor House, Shottery, sketched by Blight in the year 1865.

995. The House in Stratford-upon-Avon in which Shakspeare was born. R. Greene del. Published by Malone in 1780.

996. Exterior View of the Birth-Place. D. Parkes del., July 4th, 1806. J. Basire sculp.

997. Shakspeare's Birth-Place as it appeared at the time of the Jubilee. Fahey lithog. Published by J. Ward. 1827.

998. The Birth-Place of Shakespeare. London, Published by G. Hodgson.

999. The old timbered Court-House at Aston Cantlow. A pen-and-ink drawing by Captain Saunders, 1825

1000-1003. Sketches by Blight and Fairholt of objects at Stratford-on-Avon and Aylesbury.

1004. Charlecote House. Drawn by J. P. Neale. Engraved by W. Radclyffe. October, 1820.

1005. Charlecote House. A. E. Everitt del.

1006—1030. Sketches by Blight, taken in 1863, 1864 and 1865, and nearly all original, of objects at Charlecote, Shottery, Milcote and Stratford-on-Avon.

1031. The Tithe Barn in the Guildpits, Stratford-on-Avon, frequently used as a theatre. A pen-and-ink drawing by R. B. Wheler.

1032. Grove Field, Warwickshire, absurdly supposed to be connected with the poaching exploit. Drawn by W. Jackson, 1798. A recent lithographic copy.

1033. Westminster Abbey; Westminster Hall; Pell Mall. A curious etching by Hollar, c. 1650.

1034—1045. Sketches, chiefly original, taken by Blight in 1863 and 1865, of objects at Wilmecote, Charlecote, Shottery,

Stratford-on-Avon and Grendon Underwood.

1046. Henley-in-Arden. F. W. Fairholt, 1854.

1047—1058. Sketches, taken by Blight in 1863 and 1864, of objects at Barton-on-the-Heath, Stratford-on-Avon, Weston-on-Avon, Snitterfield, Uxbridge, Welford, Clifford Chambers, Luddington and Bishopton.

1059. Exterior of Anne Hathaway's Cottage, as it appeared about the year 1830. An engraving with neither date nor name of artist.

1060. An old timbered house at Bearley. Sketched by Blight.

1061. A plan of London by F. Valegio, c. 1550.

1062. An attic in the house in Wood Street formerly occupied by the Hathaways. Blight, 1864.

1063. Old timbered barn at Wilmecote. Sketched by Blight, 1863.

1064. A large ground-plan of the Church and Churchyard at Stratford-on-Avon, taken about the year 1800.

1065. Exterior of the Birth-Place. Another and finer impression of No. 580, with trifling variations, presented to me by Dr. Ingleby.

1066. Anne Hathaway's Cottage. Drawn from Nature and on Stone by J. Brandard, Leamington. Published by C. Elston, 12, Lower Union Parade.—Presented to me by Dr. Ingleby.

1067. A portrait of Sir William Davenant, the poet's Godson. Jo. Greenhill pinx. W. Faithorne sculp.

1068. Front of the Crown Inn, Oxford, a sketch taken by Blight in 1864.

1069. A Perspective View of the New Place, the Residence of Shakspeare, with the Chapel, Gild Hall and Alms Houses, with part of the Falcon Inn. John Jordan of Stratford del., 1793.

1070. A view of part of old Stratford from the Evesham road. Dogs in the foreground. Jordan, 1793.

These quaint drawings are taken from what was otherwise a worthless folio manuscript in my possession entitled,—" Stanzas on the Shakespeare Hunt at Stratford-upon-Avon, December the 2nd, 1793, illustrated with notes and embelished with drawings; humbly inscribed to Charles Henry Hunt esq. by John Jordan."

1071. A large and curious plan by Jordan of Stratford-on-Avon and its neighbourhood, c. 1790. In the corners are views of the Church and Guild Chapel.

1072. 1073. The Room in which Shakspere was born, and the exterior of the Birth-Place. Two lithographs "drawn from Nature on stone," by J. Brandard. Leamington, Published by C. Elston, 12, Lower Union Parade.

1074. Anne Hathaway's Cottage, an unfinished sketch taken by Blight in 1864.

1075. A view of the Falcon Inn and Church Street, Stratford-on-Avon, by Captain Saunders. Presented to me by Samuel Timmins, esq., J.P., F.S.A.

1076. A full length portrait of King James the First on his throne, with verses underneath that have been attributed to Shakespeare. Simon Passæus sculpsit, London. John Bill excudit.

1077. Miserere Seats in the Chancel of Holy Trinity Church, Stratford-on-Avon, from original sketches by H. B. Clements.

1078. A ground-plan of the Birth-Place. W.

Hemings delin. C. F. Green lithog. 1824.

1079. Original tracings made by the elder Ireland, c. 1790, of the water-marks upon the paper on which Shakespeare's will is written.

1080. A large view of the Guild Chapel, 1807.

1081. A Mappe of the County of Worcester, c. 1650.

1082. Shakespeare's Cliff, a large wood-engraving from the Saturday Magazine of April 15th, 1837.

1083. The Bridge House and old houses at Rochester, 1778.

1084. An old house in the Blackfriars erroneously said to have been Shakespeare's. Sketched by Blight, 1866.

1085. Plan of the Town and Borough of Stratford-on-Avon, engraved by J. Tolley, Birmingham. Published by J. Ward, Stratford. W. R. Swanwick, Surveyor.

1086. The Cock and Pye, a very curious old sign at Bewdley. Blight, 1867.

1087. 1088. The Golden Lion and the White

Lion Inns at Stratford-on-Avon, copies of sketches by Captain Saunders.

1089. A sign in stone carving of the George and Dragon Inn, Snow Hill, London, a work of the seventeenth century preserved in the wall of the inn and sketched by Blight in July, 1864.

1090. Vera Effigies Doctissimi Poetarum Anglorvm Ben: Iohnsonii. Ro: Vaughan fecit. 1640.

1091. A diminutive view of London showing the old theatres, from the title-page of the Cambridge edition of the Bible, 1648.

1092. Shakspere's House, Stratford-on-Avon. Exterior. A wood-engraving by Bonner.

1093. The proof impression of the Droeshout engraved portrait of Shakespeare, 1623. An account of this invaluable representation of the great dramatist will be found in the Preface.

J. G. Bishop, Printer, "Herald" Office, Brighton.

www.ingramcontent.com/pod-product-compliance
Lightning Source LLC
Chambersburg PA
CBHW020155170426
43199CB00010B/1049